WINTER

Snowy, Flowy, Blowy,
Showery, Flowery, Bowery,
Hoppy, Croppy, Droppy,
Breezy, Sneezy, Freezy.

GEORGE ELLIS (1753-1815),
'*The Twelve Months*'

WINTER

A BRITISH MUSEUM
COMPANION

EDITED BY

Marjorie Caygill

THE BRITISH MUSEUM PRESS

For Sophie, Nathan, Marc and Louis

Photography by the British Museum Department
of Photography and Imaging

A catalogue record for this book is available from the British Library

ISBN 0 7141 5033-9

Frontispiece: Aukusti Tuhka (1895-1973), *Aurora Borealis*.
Woodcut, Finland, 1917.

Designed and typeset in Centaur by Peter Ward
Printed in China by C&C Offset

INTRODUCTION

'A sad tale's best for winter', wrote William Shakespeare in the *Winter's Tale*. Less bleakly, in *As You Like It*, Adam declares, 'my age is as a lusty winter, / Frosty, but kindly'. Winter is thus a season of contrasts – the weather harsh but sometimes beautiful, the cold outside made bearable by the warmth of human contact indoors and the jollity of the festivals with which different cultures enliven the season.

The texts in this winter anthology have been drawn from diverse sources, ranging from Egypt in the second millennium BC to twentieth-century Australia by way, among others, of the Roman Empire, medieval France and nineteenth-century Japan. There are popular favourites and some less well known. The illustrations, all of which are taken from the world-wide collections of the British Museum, have been chosen to provide an appropriate accompaniment.

Some links between text and image are obvious, others are more subtle. The simpering 18th-century maiden skating with her fiancé (no. 4) is, for example, set against the sonorous words of misogynist Scandinavian gods warning against ice and women (no. 3). Both the first-century AD Roman poet Ovid and the twentieth-century inhabitants of the Atlas Mountains appreciate the advantages of warm trousers in cold weather (nos 31 and 32). Robert Frost's evocative description of snow-covered woods in New Hampshire is well suited to a modern depiction of farmland near Oslo (nos 1 and 2).

The *Winter Companion* is not just for winter. It is intended as a diversion at other seasons. The poet Lord Byron (1788-1824) described the English winter as 'ending in July, / To recommence in August'.

1. *Stopping by woods on a snowy evening*

Whose woods these are I think I know.
His house is in the village, though;
He will not see me stopping here
To watch his woods fill up with snow.

My little horse must think it queer
To stop without a farmhouse near
Between the woods and frozen lake
The darkest evening of the year.

He gives his harness bells a shake
To ask if there is some mistake.
The only other sound's the sweep
Of easy wind and downy flake.

The woods are lovely, dark, and deep.
But I have promises to keep,
And miles to go before I sleep,
And miles to go before I sleep.

ROBERT FROST (1874-1963)
USA

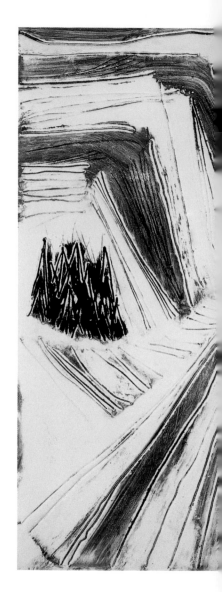

2. Rolf Nesch (1893-1975), *Skaugum*.
Metal print, Norway, 1933-4.

3. *Sayings of the High One (Hávamál)*

At evening should the day be praised,
the woman when she is cremated,

the blade when it is tested,
the girl when she is married,

the ice when it is crossed,
the ale when it is drunk.

From *The Poetic Edda*, translated by C. Larrington
Viking Age

4. Adam Buck (1759-1833), *Skating lovers.*
Aquatint by Piercy Roberts (*fl.* 1795-1828)
and J. C. Stadler (*fl.* 1780-1824), 1800.

The month of Pausha

In the month of Pausha nobody likes cold things, whether they are water, food, dress or house. Even the earth and sky have become cold. In this season everyone, rich and poor alike, likes oil (massage of oil), cotton (cotton filled clothes), betel, fire (to warm the room), sun-shine and company of young women. (During the month) the days are short and nights are dark and long. This is not the time to quarrel with one's lover . . . Keeping all these aspects in mind the Beloved asks her Lover not to leave her in the month of Pausha.

KESHAVDASA, *Barahmasa* (The Song of the Seasons)
Rajasthan, India, 17th century

6. *The cold month of Pausha.* Bundi school,
Rajasthan, India, *c.* 1675-1700.

7. *Winter scene*

Zeus rains upon us, and from the sky comes down
enormous winter. Rivers have turned to ice . . .

Dash down the winter. Throw a log on the fire
and mix the flattering wine (do not water it
    too much) and bind on round our foreheads
        soft ceremonial wreaths of spun fleece.

We must not let our spirits give way to grief.
By being sorry we get no further on,
    my Bukchis. Best of all defences
        is to mix plenty of wine, and drink it.

ALCAEUS OF MYTILENE (*c.* 620 - *c.* 580 BC),
translated by Richmond Lattimore
Greece

8. Detail from a Greek red-figured *kylix* (drinking cup) showing boys serving wine. Made in Athens *c.* 480 BC and signed by Douris as painter. Said to be from Vulci, Italy.

9. *The northern cold*

The sky glows one side black, three sides purple.
The Yellow River's ice closes, fish and dragons die.
Bark three inches thick cracks across the grain,
Carts a hundred piculs heavy mount the river's water.
Flowers of frost on the grass are as big as coins,
Brandished swords will not pierce the foggy sky,
Crashing ice flies in the swirling seas,
And cascades hang noiseless in the mountains, rainbows
    of jade.

Li Ho (AD 791-817), translated by A. C. Graham
China

10. Luke Clennel, *The Frost Fair on the River
Thames, February 4th 1814.* Etching, 1814

11. *When icicles hang by the wall*

When icicles hang by the wall,
    And Dick the shepherd blows his nail,
And Tom bears logs into the hall,
    And milk comes frozen home in pail,
When blood is nipp'd and ways be foul,
Then nightly sings the staring owl,
                      Tu-who;
Tu-whit, tu-who — a merry note,
While greasy Joan doth keel the pot.

When all aloud the wind doth blow,
    And coughing drowns the parson's saw,
And birds sit brooding in the snow,
    And Marian's nose looks red and raw,
When roasted crabs hiss in the bowl,
Then nightly sings the staring owl,
                      Tu-who;
Tu-whit, tu-who — a merry note,
While greasy Joan doth keel the pot.

WILLIAM SHAKESPEARE (1564-1616)

12. Jim Dine (b. 1935), *White owl (for Alan)*.
Cardboard intaglio etching, USA, 1995.

A Sparrow in Winter

Prior to his conversion to Christianity by St Paulinus in AD 627
King Edwin of Northumbria summoned his nobles and asked if
they too wished to be converted. One replied:

This is how the present life of man on earth, King, appears to me in comparison with that time which is unknown to us. You are sitting feasting with your ealdormen and thegns in winter time; the fire is burning on the hearth in the middle of the hall and all inside is warm, while outside the wintry storms of rain and snow are raging; and a sparrow flies swiftly through the hall. It enters in at one door and quickly flies out through the other. For the few moments it is inside, the storm and wintry tempest cannot touch it, but after the briefest moment of calm, it flits from your sight, out of the wintry storm and into it again. So this life of man appears but for a moment; what follows or indeed what went before, we know not at all. If this new doctrine brings us more certain information, it seems right that we should accept it.

The Venerable Bede (AD 673-735)

14. Pair of aurochs' horns with silver gilt mounts, used as drinking vessels. Anglo-Saxon, late 6th century AD.

15. *Haiku*

andon no   susuke zo samuki   yuki no kure

    The night-light is smoke-stained,
Snow falls chill
    Through the dusk.

ETSUJIN (1857-1936), translated by R. H. Blyth
Japan

16. Kawase Hasui (1883-1957), *Shiobara*.
Woodblock print, Japan, 1946.

January 1785

Jan. 1. Much snow on the ground. Ponds frozen-up & almost dry. Moles work: cocks crow. Ground soft under the snow. No field-fares seen; no wag-tails. Ever-greens miserably scorched; even ivy, in warm aspects.

Jan. 3. Began the new rick: the hay is very fine. Tho' my ever-greens are almost destroyed; Mr Yalden's bays, & laurels, & laurustines seem untouched. Berberries, & haws frozen on the trees. No birds eat the former . . .

Jan. 7. Shook the snow from the ever-greens, & shovelled the walks. Snow-scenes very beautiful! On this day Mr Blanchard, & Dr Jeffries rose in a balloon from Dover-cliff, & passing over the channel towards France, landed in the forest De Felmores, just 12 miles up into the country. These are the first aeronauts that have dared to take a flight over the Sea!!!

Jan. 8. Received five gallons, & seven pints of French brandy from Mr Edm^d Woods.

Jan. 11. Men begin to plough again.

Jan. 21. Made a seedling-cucumber-bed. The glazier mended the light of the seedling-frame broken by the hail.

Jan. 23. Boys play on the Plewstor at marbles, & peg-top. Thrushes sing in the coppices. Thrushes & blackbirds are much reduced.

Gilbert White (1720-93)

18. George Baxter (1804-67), *Winter*.
'Baxter' print, 1851.

19. *Now winter nights enlarge*

Now winter nights enlarge
The number of their hours;
And clouds their storms discharge
Upon the airy towers.
Let now the chimneys blaze!
And cups o'erflow with wine!
Let well-tuned words amaze,
With harmony divine!
Now yellow waxen lights
Shall wait on honey love;
While youthful revels, masques, and Courtly sights,
Sleep's leaden spells remove.

This time doth well dispense,
With lovers long discourse;
Much speech hath some defence,
Though beauty no remorse.
All do not all things well;
Some measures comely tread,
Some knotted riddles tell,
Some poems smoothly read.
The summer hath his joys,
And winter his delights;
Though love and all his pleasures are but toys,
They shorten tedious nights.

THOMAS CAMPION (1567-1620)

24

20. *'To gladden this, our New Year's Day.'* One of a collection of Christmas and New Year cards given to Queen Mary (1867-1953) and other members of the royal family between 1873 and 1953.

21. *O Tannenbaum (O Christmas tree)*

O Tannenbaum, O Tannenbaum, wie grün sind deine Blätter!
Du grünst nicht nur zur Sommerszeit, nein, auch im Winter, wenn es
   schneit,
O Tannenbaum, O Tannenbaum, wie grün sind deine Blätter!

O Tannenbaum, O Tannenbaum, du kannst mir sehr gefallen.
Wie oft hat nicht zur Weinachtszeit ein Baum von dir mich hoch
   erfreut.
O Tannenbaum, O Tannenbaum, du kannst mir sehr gefallen.

O Tannenbaum, O Tannenbaum, dein Kleid will mich was lehren:
Die Hoffnung und Beständigkeit gibt Trost und Kraft zu jeder Zeit.
O Tannenbaum, O Tannenbaum, dein Kleid will mich was lehren.

August Zarnack (1820), Ernst Anschütz (1824)
Germany

22. Albrecht Dürer (1471-1528), *A spruce tree (Picea abies)*.
   Watercolour, Germany, *c.* 1506.

23. *A song for England*

> An' a so de rain a-fall
> An' a so de snow a-rain
>
> An' a so de fog a-fall
> An' a so de sun a-fail
>
> An' a so de seasons mix
> An' a so de bag-o-tricks
>
> But a so me understan'
> De misery o' de Englishman.

ANDREW SALKEY (1928-95)
Jamaica

24. The British Museum under snow, 1991.

London snow

When men were all asleep the snow came flying,
In large white flakes falling on the city brown,
Stealthily and perpetually settling and loosely lying,
　　Hushing the latest traffic of the drowsy town;
Deadening, muffling, stifling its murmurs failing;
Lazily and incessantly floating down and down:
　　Silently sifting and veiling road, roof and railing;
Hiding difference, making unevenness even,
Into angles and crevices softly drifting and sailing.
　　All night it fell, and when full inches seven
It lay in the depth of its uncompacted lightness,
Its clouds blew off from a high and frosty heaven;
　　And all woke earlier for the unaccustomed brightness
Of the winter dawning, the strange unheavenly glare:
The eye marvelled — marvelled at the dazzling whiteness;
　　The ear hearkened to the stillness of the solemn air;
No sound of wheel rumbling nor of foot falling,
And the busy morning cries came thin and spare.
　　Then boys I heard, as they went to school, calling,
They gathered up the crystal manna to freeze
Their tongues with tasting, their hands with snowballing;
　　Or rioted in a drift, plunging up to the knees;
Or peering up from under the white-mossed wonder,
'O look at the trees!' they cried, 'O look at the trees!'
　　With lessened load a few carts creak and blunder,
Following along the white deserted way,

26. George Scharf Snr (1788-1860), *A snowball fight.*
Watercolour, 19th century.

A country company long dispersed asunder:
   When now already the sun, in pale display
Standing by Paul's high dome, spread forth below
His sparkling beams, and awoke the stir of the day.
   For now doors open, and war is waged with the snow;
And trains of sombre men, past tale of number,
Tread long brown paths, as toward their toil they go:
   But even for them awhile no cares encumber
Their minds diverted; the daily word unspoken,
The daily thoughts of labour and sorrow slumber
At the sight of the beauty that greets them, for the charm
   they have broken.

ROBERT BRIDGES (1844-1930)

27. *The grass on the mountain*

Oh, long, long
The snow has possessed the mountains.

The deer have come down and the big-horn,
They have followed the Sun to the south
To feed on the mesquite pods and the bunch grass.
Loud are the thunder drums
In the tents of the mountains.

Oh, long, long
Have we eaten *chia* seeds
And dried deer's flesh of the summer killing.
We are wearied of our huts
And the smoky smell of our garments.

We are sick with desire of the sun
And the grass on the mountain.

MARY AUSTIN (1868-1934)
Paiute, USA

28. John White (*fl.* 1583-93),
Old Indian man of Pomeiooc in winter clothing.
Watercolour, America.

The aged man in his wynter garment.

The Nativity Play

Hello, Mrs Binton. I'm so glad you could get along to see a rehearsal of our Nativity Play! . . .

Now, my Wise Men here, please!
Billy, Peter and George . . .
Now my Kings, please.

Of course, Mrs Binton, we know that by tradition the Wise Men and the Kings are one and the same, but we did want everyone in our Nursery School Nativity Play to have a chance, so we have taken a few liberties, and I don't think any one will mind.

Now Kings: Sidney, Neville, Cliff and Nikolas Anoniodes.

Four Kings, I'm afraid. We happen to have four lovely crowns, so it seemed a pity not to use them.

Sidney, put your crown on straight please, not over one eye . . .
Cliff, put your crown on, please.
It's too big? Let's see. Ah, yes it is . . .
Where are you! Oh, there you are! Nice to see you again! Change with Nikolas.
Nikolas, you can manage a big crown, can't you? You've got just the ears for it. I think if you pull your ears down a bit that will hold it up. And lean back a bit. That's it.
Stay like that, dear. Don't move.
Wise Men and Kings, don't muddle yourselves with each other.

JOYCE GRENFELL (1910-79)

30. Rembrandt van Rijn (1606-69), *The star of the Kings.*
Pen and ink drawing, The Netherlands, c. 1645-7.

31. *Winter at Tomi*

The snow lies deep: nor sun nor melting shower
Serves to abate the winter's icy power.
One fall has scarcely come another's there,
And stays in drifts unmelted all the year.
Fierce and tempestuous is the North-wind's sway;
It levels towers of stone and carries roofs away.

With skins and trousers men keep out the cold;
Naught but their faces can your eyes behold.
Into one mass their hair is frozen tight,
Their beards with hoary rime hang glistening white.
Nor need they jars their liquor to confine,
They do not quaff a cup, they break a bit of wine.

Water is brittle here; you use a spade;
And running streams by frost are solid made.
Even the Danube flows with waves concealed
The dark blue surface into ice congealed.
On foot we go across the unmoving tide
And horses' hoofs ring loud where once their oarsmen plied.

OVID (43 BC - AD 18), translated by F. A. Wright
Roman Empire

32. Man's knitted woollen trousers.
Morocco, 1968.

33. *From 'The shooting of Dan McGrew'*

Were you ever out in the Great Alone,
    when the moon was awful clear,
And the icy mountains hemmed you in
    with a silence you most could *hear*;
With only the howl of the timber wolf,
    and you camped there in the cold,
A half-dead thing in a stark, dead world,
    clean mad for the muck called gold;
While high overhead, green, yellow and red,
    the North Lights swept in bars —
Then you've a hunch what the music meant . . .
    hunger and night and the stars.

ROBERT W. SERVICE (1874-1958)
Canada

34. Félix Bracquemond (1833-1914), *Hiver (le loup dans la neige)*.
Etching, France, 1864.

35. *Ballade des dames de temps jadis*
(Where are the snows of yesteryear?)

Dictes moy ou, n'en quel pays,
Est Flora, la belle Rommaine,
Archipiades, ne Thaïs,
Qui fut sa cousine germaine,
Echo parlant quant bruyt ou maine
Dessus riviere ou sus estan,
Qui beaulté ot trop plus qu'humaine.
Mais ou sont les neiges d'antan?

Ou est la tres sage Helloïs
Pour qui chastré fut et puis moyne
Pierre Esbaillart a Saint-Denis?
Pour son amour ot ceste essoyne.
Semblablement, ou est la royne
Qui commanda que Buridan
Fust geté en ung sac en Saine?
Mais ou sont les neiges d'antan?

La royne Blanche comme lis
Qui chantoit a voix de seraine,
Berte au grand pié, Beatris, Alis,
Haremburgis qui tint le Maine,
Et Jehanne, la bonne Lorraine,
Qu'Englois brulerent a Rouan;
Où sont ilz, ou, Vierge souvraine?
Mais ou sont les neiges d'antan?

Prince, n'enquerez de sepmaine
Ou elles sont, ne de cest an,
Qu'a ce reffrain ne vous remaine:
Mais ou sont les neiges d'antan?

FRANÇOIS VILLON (1431-63?)
France

36. Shunkyokusai Hokumei
(*fl. c.* 1818-44), *Tokiwa Gozen with her sons
in the snow*. Hanging scroll, ink and
colour on silk, Japan.

The Traditions of Midwinter Greenery

The use of evergreen plants to decorate houses at the midwinter solstice is a custom which long antedates Christianity in Europe and Asia. Evergreens, flourishing when all other plant life seems dead or dormant, were regarded as symbols of the continuity of life through the dark season.

In ancient Rome, for example, garlands were made from Mediterranean bay, box, rosemary, pines and evergreen oak. In Britain the native holly, ivy and mistletoe were (and still are) the favoured plants . . . they were often used together, in wreaths hung on the door or over the porch, for instance. A favourite decoration in late medieval England was the kissing bough, which was a garland of greenery shaped roughly like a crown and adorned with fruit, coloured paper rosettes, candles, and most importantly, a bunch of mistletoe hanging from the centre.

There have been strict rules about when the midwinter greenery should be put up, when it should be taken down, and how it should be disposed of. Twelfth Night (6 January) has long been a watershed. But in some areas the greenery was kept until Candlemas Eve. In some it was ceremonially burned, in others fed as a charm to cattle. Most of these local customs have faded and been absorbed into the national pattern. But there are still places where the rituals associated with midwinter greenery kept a distinctive local flavour until recently.

RICHARD MABEY (b. 1941)

38. Mary Delany (1700-88),
White mistletoe (Viscum album).
Paper collage, December 1776.

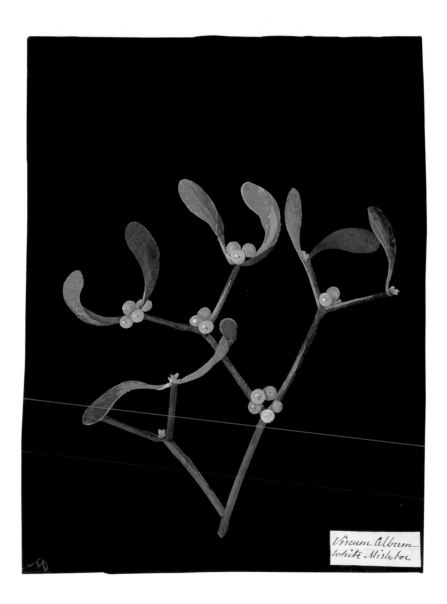

Viscum Album
White Mistletoe

43

39. *I sing of a maiden*

I sing of a maiden
That is makeles:
King of alle kinges
To here sone she ches.

He cam also stille
Ther his moder was,
As dew in Aprille
That falleth on the grass.

He cam also stille
To his moderes bowr,
As dew in Aprille
That falleth on the flowr.

He cam also stille
Ther his moder lay,
As dew in Aprille
That falleth on the spray.

Moder and maiden
Was never non but she;
Well may swich a lady
Godes moder be.

ANONYMOUS, early 15th century

40. The Madonna and Child trampling on the devil.
Ivory, France, *c.* 1325-30.

And numerous indeed are the hearts to which Christmas brings a brief season of happiness and enjoyment. How many families whose members have been dispersed and scattered far and wide, in the restless struggles of life, are then re-united, and meet once again in that happy state of companionship and mutual good-will, which is a source of such pure and unalloyed delight, and one so incompatible with the cares and sorrows of the world, that the religious belief of the most civilised nations, and the rude traditions of the roughest savages, alike number it among the first joys of a future state of existence, provided for the blest and happy! How many old recollections, and how many dormant sympathies, does Christmas time awaken!

. . . Happy, happy Christmas, that can win us back to the delusions of our childish days, that can recall to the old man the pleasures of his youth, and transport the sailor and the traveller, thousands of miles away, back to his own fire-side and his quiet home!

CHARLES DICKENS (1812-70)

42. Unknown artist,
Winter fashions for 1838 and 1839.
Aquatint, 1838.

43. *Christmas family reunion*

Since last the tutelary hearth
　　Has seen this bursting pod of kin,
I've thought how good the family mould,
　　How solid and how genuine.

Now once again the aunts are here,
　　The uncles, sisters, brothers,
With candy in the children's hair,
　　The grownups in each other's.

There's talk of saving room for pie;
　　Grandma discusses her neuralgia.
I long for time to pass, so I
　　Can think of all this with nostalgia.

PETER DE VRIES (1910-93)
USA

44. Tom Hammick (b. 1963),
House in moonlight, at Christmas time.
Woodcut, 2002.

INUIT SEASONS, DESCRIBED BY
THE IGLULINGMIUT PEOPLE OF IGLOOLIK

Moon Month	Season	Celestial markers	Biological and Environmental markers	Social Activities (selected)
SIQINNAARUT 'Sun is possible' (January/February)	*UKIUQ* 'Winter'	*Aagjuuk* stars seen at dawn. Mid January Sun and Moon compete; *ingiaqautijuuk* Sun leaves the horizon; *kullutaniktuq*	Formation of *uiguaq* at the floe-edge. *Mauliq* hunting for ring seals through the *uiguaq*.	String games (*ajaraaq*) discontinued by taboo – replaced by *ajagaq*.
QANGATTAASAN 'It (the Sun) gets higher.' Also known as *Akurlungnag* (February/March).	*UKIUQ* 'Winter'	Sun rising higher 'Pualutanikpuq'	Walrus migrate towards the land-fast ice. Bearded seal shunted through the *uiguaq*.	Winter camps established on the sea ice for seal- and walrus-hunting.

JOHN MACDONALD
Nunavut, Canada, 1998

46. Barbara Hepworth (1903-75), *Winter solstice.*
Graphite, watercolour and bodycolour, 1969.

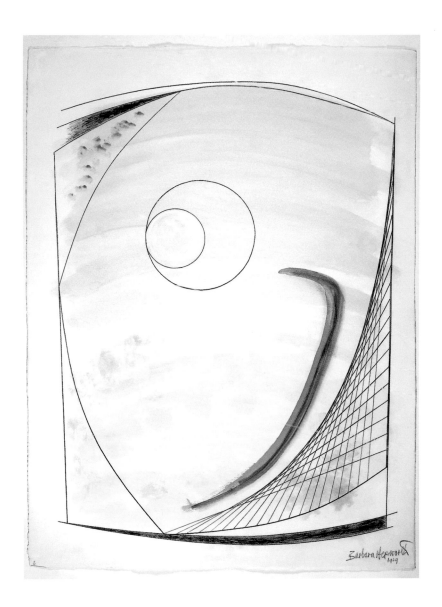

Colonel Cold strode up the Line
  (tabs of rime and spurs of ice);
stiffened all that met his glare:
  horses, men, and lice.

Visited a forward post,
  left them burning, ear to foot;
fingers stuck to biting steel,
  toes to frozen boot.

Stalked on into No Man's Land,
  turned the wire to fleecy wool,
iron stakes to sugar sticks
  snapping at a pull.

Those who watched with hoary eyes
  saw two figures gleaming there;
Hauptmann Kälte, Colonel Cold,
  gaunt in the grey air.

Stiffly, tinkling spurs they moved,
  glassy-eyed, with glinting heel
stabbing those who lingered there
  torn by screaming steel.

EDGELL RICKWORD (1898-1982)

Paul Nash 1918

48. Paul Nash (1889-1946), *Void of war*. Lithograph, 1918.

49. *Hymn to Senwosret III*

How great is the lord of his city:
lo he is an overflowing shade,
    cool in summer.

How great is the lord of his city:
lo he is a warm corner,
    dry in the wintertime.

ANONYMOUS
Egypt, *c.* 1820 BC

50. *Ploughing in the winter season.* Model from
the tomb of an Egyptian official.
Middle Kingdom, *c.* 1900 BC.

IN A SNOW DRIFT UPON MOUNT TARRAR

. . . the snow began to fall at Foligno, tho' more of ice than snow, that the coach from its weight slide about in all directions, that walking was much preferable, but my innumerable tails would not do that service so I soon got wet through and through, till at Sarre-valli the diligence zizd into a ditch and required 6 oxen, sent three miles back for, to drag it out; this cost 4 Hours, that we were 10 Hours beyond our time at Macerata, consequently half starved and frozen we at last got to Bologna . . . But there our troubles began instead of diminishing – the Milan diligence was unable to pass Placentia. We therefore hired a voiture, the horses were knocked up the first post, Sigr turned us over to another lighter carriage which put my coat in requisition night and day, for we never could keep warm or make our day's distance good, the places we put up at proved all bad till Firenzola being even the worst for the down diligence people had devoured everything eatable (Beds none) . . . crossed Mont Cenis on a sledge – bivouacked in the snow with fires lighted for 3 Hours on Mount Tarare while the diligence was righted and dug out, for a Bank of Snow saved it from upsetting – and in the same night we were again turned out to walk up to our knees in new fallen drift to get assistance to dig a channel thro' it for the coach, so that from Foligno to within 20 miles of Paris I never saw the road but snow!

J. M. W. TURNER, letter to Charles Eastlake, February 1829

52. J. M. W. Turner (1/75 1851), *Messieurs les voyageurs on their return from Italy (par la diligence) in a snow drift upon Mount Tarrar — 22nd of January 1829*. Watercolour, 1829.

53. *From 'Winter'*

Wind sharp, hillside bleak, hard to win shelter;
    Ford is impassable, lake is frozen;
   A man may near stand on one stalk of grass.

   Wave upon wave roofs over land-edge;
Shouts loud against breast of peak and brae;
    Outside, a man may barely stand.

Lake-haunts cold, with the storm winds of winter;
    Withered the reeds, stalks all broken;
   Wind-gusts angry, stripping of woods.

Cold bed of fish in the gloom of ice;
    Stag lean, bearded reeds;
   Evening brief, slant of bent wood.

Snow falls, covers with white;
Warriors go not forth on foray;
Lakes cold, their tint without sunlight.

Snow falls, hoarfrost white;
Idle shield on an old shoulder;
A monstrous wind freezes the grass.

ANONYMOUS Welsh, 10th-11th century,
translated by Tony Conran

54. A Dakota (Sioux) 'winter count' for the
years 1785 to 1901. Cotton textile, USA.

59

55.   *Winter road*

Across the wavering hazes
Moon is breaking on the sight.
Across each melancholy clearing
Pours a melancholy light.

Down the wintry dismal road
Runs the troika, and the tone
Of its tuneless sleigh-bell
Monotonously jangles on . . .

One hears the old familiar note
In the coachman's lengthy song,
Drunk carousal yielding place
To lament and lover's wrong . . .

Not a light, no darkened cabin,
Silence, snow. As I pass by
Only mileposts with their ciphers
Attend me on my endless way.

Dismal, dreary . . . but tomorrow,
Nina, returning to you there,
I shall never gaze my fill
Dreaming and gazing by the fire.

Tunefully the circling clock
Will complete its measured round,
And removing the intruders
For us that midnight will not sound.

56. Philibert Louis Debucourt after Michel Damame-Demartrais,
Preparations for a Russian sleigh ride (Isvoschtschik prêt à partir). Aquatint, France, 1806.

Dismal, Nina, drear my journey,
Quiet the coachman – sleep has won;
Monotonous the sleigh-bell's jangle,
Cloud has blotted back the moon.

ALEXANDER SERGEEVICH PUSHKIN (1799-1837),
translated by Charles Tomlinson
Russia

ASHUR-MALIK COMPLAINS TO HIS
BROTHER ASHUR-IDI

To Ashur-idi speak:

Thus said Ashur-malik: Once and twice I sent you a message and your instruction does not come. Now the cold season has actually arrived. Where is the stove? Ena-Anum is sitting in our guest-room and continually despatches me on errands. You are my brother. From there send me wool, 15 minas or 20 minas . . . Why have you shut me up in the midst of the city for ten months like a woman? And yet, here no one gives me money on security. Here the cold season has come. There is not a single piece of bread, no fire-wood, no cloth for a robe. Why shall our lot be set? From there, however, send me cloth for dressing and then let me get up and actually come. My garment, too is worn! My covering has now fallen down from me! I am locked in like a slave! Had I known these things would I have sat here until this day? Do not say thus: 'Somehow he will give you cheap wool.' He is not willing at all to give cheap wool.

Thus he said: 'Where shall I take it and then give it to you?' And yet I begged him five and six times! From there send me somehow a used garment and then let me myself come!

Cuneiform tablet, translation after J. Lewy
Assyria (c. 1920-1740 BC)

58. Ashur-malik's letter to his brother Ashur-idi (text opposite).
Clay cuneiform tablet and its envelope, from Kültepe, Central Anatolia,
1920–1740 BC. The last three lines of the text were written on an
additional sliver of clay squeezed into the envelope.

59. THE TWELVE DAYS OF CHRISTMAS

In England this memory game begins 'On the first day of
Christmas my true love sent to me'. The gifts eventually comprise:

A partridge in a pear tree, 2 turtle doves,
3 French hens, 4 colly birds, 5 gold rings,
6 geese a-laying, 7 swans a-swimming,
8 maids a-milking, 9 drummers drumming,
10 pipers piping, 11 ladies dancing,
12 lords a-leaping.

In Scotland the preamble runs 'The king sent his lady on the
first Yule day, a popingo-aye [parrot]; Wha learns my carol
and carries it away?' and the menagerie consists of:

3 partridges, 3 plovers, a goose that was grey,
3 starlings, 3 goldspinks, a bull that was brown,
3 ducks a-merry laying, 3 swans a-merry swimming,
an Arabian baboon, 3 hinds a-merry hunting,
3 maids a-merry dancing, 3 stalks o' merry corn.

In the west of France the list includes:

A good stuffing without bones, 2 breasts of veal,
3 joints of beef, 4 pigs' trotters, 5 legs of mutton,
6 partridges with cabbage, 7 spitted rabbits,
8 plates of salad, 9 dishes for a chapter of canons,
10 full casks, 11 beautiful full-breasted maidens,
12 musketeers with their swords.

TRADITIONAL

60. Unknown artist, *Ianuarius* (January). A winter feast from 'The Twelve Months'. Woodcut, France, *c.* 1580.

61. *Anglo-Saxon riddles*

(i) I was a pure girl and a grey-maned woman
and, at the same time, a singular man.
I flew with the birds, breasted the sea,
sank beneath the wave, dissolved among fish
and alighted on land. I had a living soul.

62. Maruyama Ōkyo (1733-95), *Cracked ice.*
Two-fold screen painting, Japan, 1780s.

(ii)　The wave, over the wave, a weird thing I saw,
thorough-wrought, and wonderfully ornate:
a wonder on the wave — water become bone.

TRADITIONAL

63. *Dry throat*

My throat is dry
Too sore to sing Jangala
A thick, dry throat
A bad cold grips me
The cold blocks my throat

The cold blocks my throat
Such a heavy cold
Caught from you people

Caught from you people
The cold impedes me
Such a heavy cold
With my hands, under water

With my hands, under water
I work clay, for a poultice
Caught from you people
The cold impedes me

The cold impedes me
Such a heavy cold
A thick, dry throat
And I cannot sing properly.

Jimmy Murray
Dyirbal, Australia, 1967

64. George Scharf Snr (1788-1860), *London sketches*.
Watercolour, 19th century.

65. *Lines written on a window at*
    The Leasowes at a time of a very deep snow

In this small fort, besieg'd with snow,
When ev'ry studious pulse beats low,
    What does my wish require?
Some sprightly girls beneath my roof,
Some friends sincere, and winter proof;
    A bottle and a fire.

Prolong, O snow! prolong thy siege!
With these, thou wilt but more oblige,
    And bless me with thy stay;
Extend, extend, thy frigid reign,
My few *sincerer friends* detain;
    And keep *false friends* away.

WILLIAM SHENSTONE (1714-63)

A glad New Year to you.

66. New Year card sent to Queen Mary,
then Princess Mary of Teck, in 1889.

67.   *On change of weathers*

And were it for thy profit, to obtaine
All *Sunshine?* No vicissitude of *Raine?*
Thinkst thou, that thy laborious *Plough* requires
Not Winter *frosts*, as well as Summer *fiers?*
There must be both: Sometimes these hearts of ours
Must have the sweet, the seasonable Showres
Of *Teares*; Sometimes the Frost of chill *despaire*
Makes our desired *sunshine* seeme more *faire*:
Weathers that most oppose the Flesh and Blood,
Are such as helpe to make our *Harvest* good:
We may not choose, great *God*: It is thy *Task*:
We know not what to *have*; nor how to ask.

FRANCIS QUARLES (1592-1644)

68. *Marble statue of Demeter*. Greece, *c.* 350 BC.
Persephone, daughter of the goddess Demeter, was abducted by Hades,
King of the Underworld. Eventually mother and daughter were reunited,
but because during her absence Persephone had eaten some pomegranate
seeds she was obliged to return to Hades for part of each year. While she
was away Demeter mourned and the earth experienced winter.

69. *After the winter*

Some day, when trees have shed their leaves
    And against the morning's white
The shivering birds beneath the eaves
    Have sheltered for the night,
We'll turn our faces southward, love,
    Toward the summer isle
Where bamboos spire to shafted grove
    And wide-mouthed orchids smile.

And we will seek the quiet hill
    Where towers the cotton tree,
And leaps the laughing crystal rill
    And works the droning bee,
And we will build a cottage there
    Beside an open glade,
With black-ribbed blue-bells blowing near
    And ferns that never fade.

CLAUDE MCKAY (1889-1948)
Jamaica

70. Card sent by Queen Victoria to her future granddaughter-in-law
Princess Mary of Teck, 1 January 1892: '*To dear Mary Teck. May these flowers from
the Highlands bring you good luck and every blessing, from her devoted Grandmama.*'

71. *I saw three ships*

I saw three ships come sailing by,
    Come sailing by, come sailing by,
I saw three ships come sailing by,
    On New-Year's day in the morning.

And what do you think was in them then,
    Was in them then, was in them then?
And what do you think was in them then,
    On New-Year's day in the morning?

Three pretty girls were in them then,
    Were in them then, were in them then,
Three pretty girls were in them then,
    On New-Year's day in the morning.

One could whistle, and one could sing,
    And one could play on the violin;
Such joy there was at my wedding,
    On New-Year's day in the morning.

TRADITIONAL

72. Walter Crane (1845-1915), *I saw three ships*.
Illustration to 'Baby's Opera'.
Watercolour over woodcut, 1877.

I·SAW·

THREE·SHIPS

77

73. *The jester*

'In October what is your diet?'
Thou shalt dine on spoiled oil in onions,
    and goose pluckings in porridge.

'In November what is your diet?'
Thou shalt dine on pod-weed in turnips,
    and "cleanser-plant" in crowfoot.

'In December what is your diet?'
Thou shalt dine on wild donkey dung in bitter garlic,
    and emmer chaff in sour milk.

'In January what is your diet?'
Thou shalt dine on goose eggs and dung embedded in sand,
    and cumin infused with Euphrates water in ghee.

ANONYMOUS Neo-Assyrian satirical dialogue, *c.* 650 BC

74. Mask worn by the *Nulthamalth,* or fool dancer, in the
winter ceremonies of the Kwakwaka'wakw people.
Canada (Northwest Coast), 19th century.

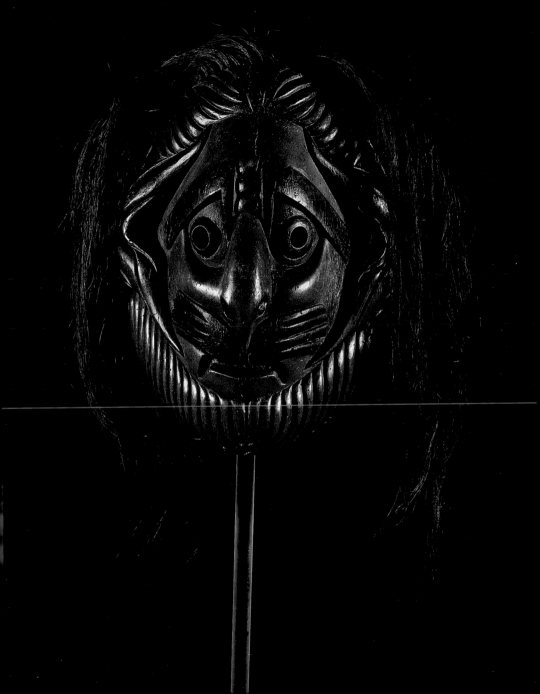

75. *The trees*

In their nakedness
the winter trees laugh
at our inability
to shed the clothes
of our past seasons.

CHARLES MUNGOSHI (b. 1947)
Zimbabwe

76. Porcelain seal paste box decorated in overglaze enamels.
Made by Xu Naijing, Jingdezhen, China, 1937.

今
夜
誰
家
一
舟
子

明
朝
護
得
十
分
春

丁
丑
春
月
畫

可
聲
先
生
清
玩

許
人
何
菊
畫
於

盂
浦
敬
婣

It is now December, & hee that walkes the streets, shall find durt on his shooes, Except hee goe all in bootes: Now doth the Lawyer make an end of his harvest, and the Client of his purse: Now Capons and Hennes, beside Turkies, Geese and Duckes, besides Beefe and Mutton, must all die for the great feast, for in twelve dayes a multitude of people will not bee fed with a little: Now plummes and spice, Sugar and Honey, square it among pies and broth, and Gossip I drinke to you, and you are welcome, and I thanke you, and how doe you, and I pray you bee merrie: Now are the Taylors and the Tiremakers [dressmakers] full of worke against the Holidayes, and Musicke now must bee in tune, or else never: the youth must dance and sing, and the aged sit by the fire. It is the Law of Nature, and no contradiction in reason: The Asse that hath borne all the yeare, must now take a little rest, and the lean Oxe must feed till he bee fat The Footman now shall have many a foule step, and the Ostler shall have worke enough about the heeles of the Horses, while the Tapster, if hee take not heed, will lie drunke in the Seller: The prices of meat will rise apace, and the apparell of the proud will make the Taylor rich: Dice and Cards will benefit the Butler: And if the Cooke doe not lacke wit, hee will sweetly licke his fingers: Starchers and Launderers will have their hands full of worke, and Periwigs and painting wil not bee a little set by, Strange Stuffes will bee well sold, Strange tales well told, Strange sights much sought, Strange things much bought, and what else as fals out. To conclude, I hold it the costly Purveyour of Excesse, and the after breeder of necessitie, the practice of Folly, and the Purgatory of Reason.
Farewell.

NICHOLAS BRETON (1545?-1626)

The cold, not cruelty makes her weare   *Winter*   For a smoother skinn at night
In Winter, furrs and Wild beasts haire   Embraceth her with more delight.

78. Wenceslaus Hollar (1607-77), *Winter*. Etching, 1643.

79. *Winter is a dreary season*

Winter is a dreary season,
Heavy waters in confusion
    Beat the wide world's strand.
Birds of every place are mournful
But the hot and savage ravens,
    At rough winter's shriek.
Crude and black and dank and smoky;
Dogs about their bones are snarling,
On the fire the cauldron bubbles
    All the long dark day.

ANONYMOUS Irish, 7th-13th century,
translated by Frank O'Connor

荒陂三家夜秋風箏
墨情邵和河愛雁然
後反本聲
癸亥秋仲
聲龍山人月田

80. Chang Wu-song (b. 1912), *Flying cranes.*
Ink and colours on paper, Korea, 1994.

81. *Up in the morning early*

> Up in the morning's no for me,
>   Up in the morning early;
> When a' the hills are cover'd wi' snaw,
>   I'm sure it's winter fairly.

Cold blaws the wind frae east to west,
    The drift is driving sairly;
Sae loud and shrill's I hear the blast,
    I'm sure it's winter fairly.

The birds sit chittering in the thorn,
    A' day they fare but sparely;
And lang's the night frae e'en to morn,
    I'm sure it's winter fairly.

> Up in the morning's no for me,
>   Up in the morning early;
> When a' the hills are cover'd wi' snaw,
>   I'm sure it's winter fairly.

ROBERT BURNS (1759-96)

82. Miroslav Holý (1897-1974), *Clearing snow.*
Lithograph, Czechoslovakia, 1924.

86

83. *Love ever green*

Grene growth the holy,
So doth the ivy.
Thow winter blastes blow never so hye,
Grene growth the holy.

As the holy growth grene
And never chaungeth hew,
So I am, ever hath bene,
Unto my lady trew.

As the holy growth grene
With ivy all alone,
When floweres cannot be sene
And grenewode leves be gone,

Now unto my lady
Promise to her I make,
Frome all other only
To her I me betake.

Adew! mine owne lady,
Adew! my speciall,
Who hath my hart, trewly,
Be suere, and ever shall.

Attributed to HENRY VIII
(1491-1547), *c.* 1515

84. Mary Delany (1700-88),
Holly with berries (Ilex aquifolium).
Paper collage, November 1775.

Ilex Aquifolium.
Holly

NOTES ON THE TEXT AND ILLUSTRATIONS

Frontispiece: PD 1939-7-30-86. Given by the Contemporary Art Society. © DACS 2004.

1. Robert Frost's poetry is evocative of the farm country of New Hampshire, USA, where he lived. From *The Poetry of Robert Frost*, ed. Edward Connery Lathem, Henry Holt & Company, New York, 1923, and Jonathan Cape, London, 1972. © 1923, 1969 by Henry Holt & Company, © 1951 by Robert Frost. Reprinted by permission of Henry Holt and Company, LLC, the Estate of Robert Frost and the Random House Group Ltd.

2. From the 'Snow Series' depicting the landscape around Oslo, produced soon after the artist's flight from Nazi Germany. 'Skaugum' is the name of a farm, the residence of the Norwegian Crown Prince. PD 1994-5-15-40. Purchased from the Rausing Fund. © DACS 2004.

3. *Hávamál* is a series of versified stories of the gods of the North and their sayings, written down in the 13th-14th century. Some material may date from as early as the 8th or 9th centuries. From *The Poetic Edda*, trans. Carolyne Larrington, Oxford World's Classics, 1966.

4. PD 1932-10-19-1. Given by Miss F. Laura Cannan, 1931.

5. In the 'Song of the Seasons' the woman implores her lover not to leave her for a reason appropriate to the time of year. The month of *Pausha* is equivalent to December/January. From V. P. Dwivedi, *Barahmasa. The Song of Seasons in Literature and Art*, published by Agam Prasad, MA, for Agam Kala Prakashan, Delhi, 1980.

6. Krishna and Radha are seated on a terrace with a tray of betel nuts. A man is receiving an oil massage in a room off the courtyard; another awaits his turn. The sun sets in the distant horizon over a yellow landscape, indicating the dry winter months. OA 1999.12-2.0.5 (2). Anonymous gift.

7. The poet Alcaeus lived on the Greek island of Lesbos in the north-eastern Aegean during its cultural peak in the 7th and 6th centuries BC. Mytilene is the principal town. From *Greek Lyrics*, trans. Richmond Lattimore, 2nd edn, University of Chicago Press, 1960.

8. Before transfer to a *kylix*, wine might be mixed with water in a *bell-krater*. GR 1843.11-3,15.

9. Li Ho was famous in the ninth century but, since he offended the conventionality of later taste by his individuality, his reputation faded. From *Poems of the Late T'ang*, trans. A.C. Graham, Penguin Classics, Harmondsworth, 1965. © A.C. Graham 1965.

10. The medieval London Bridge was built on nineteen narrow arches that served to slow the flow of the River Thames. Until the old bridge was demolished in 1831 the river froze over during cold winters and impromptu fairs were held. PD 1880-11-13-1759.

11. *Love's Labours Lost* (Act v, Scene ii) ends with this song.

12. From an exhibition, 'Jim Dine – Winter Dream' (Alan Cristea Gallery, London, 1995). PD 1999-2-28-4. © ARS, NY and DACS, London 2004.

13. The monk Bede's *Historia Ecclesiastica Gentis Anglorum*, completed in 731, begins with the invasion of Julius Caesar. Bede lived and died in the Kingdom of Northumbria and is buried in Durham Cathedral. From *The Ecclesiastical History of the English People*, ed. Judith McClure and Roger Collins, Oxford World's Classics, 1994.

14. These vessels were discovered in a late 6th-century princely burial at Taplow, Buckinghamshire, in 1883. MME 1883,12-14,19-20. Given by Rev. Charles T. E. Whateley.

15. Etsujin conjures up the coldness evoked by the image of a small, smoky night-light (*andon*). From R.H. Blyth, *Haiku*, vol. IV, *Autumn-Winter*, Hokuseido Press, Tokyo, 1952.

16. Shiobara is a famous hot spring resort in the mountains of Tochigi Prefecture. JA 1987.3-16.0518.

17. Gilbert White was Vicar of the small village of Selborne, in Hampshire. In 1768 he began his *Naturalist's Journal*, which continued until shortly before his death. From *Journals of Gilbert White*, ed. Walter Johnson (first published Routledge, London 1931; Futura edition, Macdonald & Co., London and Sydney, 1982), ch. XVIII. Reprinted by permission of Routledge & Kegan Paul Ltd.

18. Baxter was the inventor of a method of printing in oil colours. PD 1901-11-5-33. Given by F. W. Baxter.

19. Campion was a poet, musician and doctor, author of a number of court masques. From Edward Arber, *An English Garner . . .*, vol. III, Birmingham, 1880.

20. This collection of Christmas and New Year cards was given to the British Museum by Queen Mary. Senders include Queen Victoria, Edward VII and Queen Alexandra, Queen Mary's children and grandchildren, Kaiser Wilhelm II of Germany and the Russian Tsarina Alexandra. PD 1947-10-11-3-41.

21. Words by Anschütz after an older poem; music by Zarnack based on a traditional tune. Green both in summer and winter, the tree is a perpetual source of delight. From *Deutsche Lieder: Texte und Melodien ausgewählt und eingeleitet von Ernst Klusen*, © Insel Verlag, Frankfurt am Main, 1980.

22. PD 1846-9-18-9.

23. Andrew Salkey, novelist, diarist and critic was born in Jamaica in 1928 and spent some time in London. From *Caribbean Voices. An Anthology of West Indian Poetry*, ed. John Figueroa, Evans Brothers, London, 1971. Reprinted courtesy of Mrs Patricia Salkey.

24. Photograph by Andrew Hamilton.

25. From the *The Shorter Poems of Robert Bridges*, George Bell & Sons, London, 1890.

26. This sketch, from a volume executed in 1828 and 1841, is annotated 'There having been a Boyes School opposite the house where the Artist lived, he had an opportunity to draw there'. PD 1900-7-25-120-34. Bequeathed by George Scharf Jnr.

27. Mary Austin moved from Illinois to California in 1888. There she acquired a considerable knowledge of the Desert Country and of the people who lived there. This is one of a number of poems derived from Native American traditions. From M. Austin, *The American Rhythm*, Harcourt, Brace & Co., New York, 1923.

28. From a collection of drawings made in the 16th century by John White at the Roanoke colony in Virginia. PD 1906-5-9-19.

29. Joyce Grenfell's monologue, dedicated to 'all who cope in Nursery schools', captures the enchanting chaos of the school nativity play. From Joyce Grenfell, *George — Don't Do That . . .*, Macmillan, London, 1977. © Joyce Grenfell 1977.

30. The drawing illustrates a Netherlandish custom, in celebration of the feast of the Epiphany (6 January) when, to commemorate the visit of the three Kings to Bethlehem, children went from door to door, asking for gifts, and carrying a lantern shaped like the star of the Kings. PD 1910-2-12-189. Bequeathed by George Salting.

31. Publius Ovidius Naso ('Ovid') is particularly known for his love poetry. This poem (*Tristia*, III, x, 13-32) was written after he was exiled to the Black Sea by the Emperor Augustus in AD 8. From Ovid, *The Lover's Handbook*, trans. F.A. Wright, Routledge & Sons, London, 1923.

32. The trousers (*tha 'ban*) are worn by hunters of the Ayt Oumalou of the High Atlas Mountains of Morocco during the cold winter season. Ethno Af 37.25 (1969).

33. Robert Service is known for his poems about the Yukon gold rush. The poem from which this extract is taken begins 'A bunch of the boys were whooping it up in the Malamute Saloon; the kid that handles the music-box was playing a jag-time tune. . .'. From Robert W. Service, *Songs of a Sourdough*, William Briggs, Toronto, 1907. By permission of the Estate of Robert Service.

34. PD 1866-2-10-207.

35. From the *Testament*, composed by Villon during the winter of 1461-2 when he was in hiding on the outskirts of Paris. A sentence of death in 1463 was commuted to banishment and Villon disappears from history. In this ballad, with its haunting refrain, the poet alludes to beautiful women of the past, among them courtesans and queens, Heloïse and her lover Abelard, and Joan of Arc, who have now vanished like snow. From *François Villon, Poésies Choisies*, ed. J. Passeron, Classiques Larousse, Paris, 1960.

36. Tokiwa Gozen, mistress of the warrior Minamoto no Yoshitomo, fled with her three sons after Yoshitomo's defeat in the Heiji war of 1159. The baby is the future warrior hero Minamoto no Yoshitsune. JA 1913.5-1.0316. Given by Sir W. Gwynne-Evans, Bt.

37. From *Flora Britannica*, Chatto & Windus, London, 1998. Used by permission of the Random House Group Limited. *Flora Britannica* is a record of the popular culture, domestic uses and social meanings of around one thousand species of British wild plants.

38. Mrs Delany's collages are made from minute pieces of coloured paper. She began these delicate works at the age of 72 and completed about one thousand before stopping in 1782 because of failing eyesight. PD 1897-5-5-895. Given by Lady Llanover.

39. A medieval English carol of the Incarnation. *Makeles*: without equal; *To here sone she ches*: she chose for her son; *also*: as; *moder*: mother; *swich*: such. British Library, MS Sloane 2590, f. 10b. This version is from *Medieval English Lyrics. A Critical Anthology*, ed. R.T. Davies, Faber, London, 1963.

40. MME 1978,5-2,3. From the estate of Sir Harold Wernher.

41. *Pickwick Papers* (Chapman & Hall, London, 1837) recounts the journeys, adventures and observations of Mr Samuel Pickwick and the Pickwick Club. This extract is from 'A good-humoured Christmas chapter' (ch. XXVIII).

42. The setting for the display of fashions is Regent's Park, London. PD 1931-11-14-357.

43. From P. de Vries, *The Tents of Wickedness*, Gollancz, London, 1959. The poem first appeared in the *New Yorker* and is reprinted by permission of Pollinger Limited and Peter de Vries.

44. Tom Hammick described his composition thus: 'an idea originally worked on for the *Big Issue*. I wanted to try to recreate the feeling of someone on the street, at night in winter, looking into the lit-up windows of a house at Christmas time. I hope the windows conjure up an advent calendar, looking through the Bridget Riley window, the Kandinsky, the Barnett Newman, the Hirst "Spot Painting" window and so on'. PD 2003-12-31-36. Given by the artist. © Tom Hammick 2004. All Rights Reserved DACS.

45. From John MacDonald, *The Arctic Sky. Inuit Astronomy, Star Lore, and Legend*. Royal Ontario Museum/© Nunavut Research Institute 1998, 2000. *Mauliq* hunting: hunting through seal breathing holes in the ice; *Uiguaq*: formation of new ice along the floe-edge; *Qangattaasan*: also a reference to the development of the snow 'cones' over the breathing holes of ring seals; *Akurlungnag*: a reference to the formation of frost between the inner and outer layers of the back flaps (*aku*) of a caribou parka, in this coldest of months.

46. PD 1973-1-20-28. © Bowness, Hepworth Estate.

47. Edgell Rickword evokes, from personal experience, the misery of winter warfare in the trenches during the First World War. First published in 1921. From *Edgell Rickword: Collected Poems*, ed. C. Hobday, Carcanet Press, Manchester, 1991.

48. The desolation of the Western Front is depicted in Nash's rainy landscape. Nash wrote of Passchendaele in November 1917, 'only the black rain out of the bruised and swollen clouds all through the bitter black of night is fit atmosphere in such a land'. PD 1918-7-4-8. Given by the artist. © Tate, London 2004.

49. From an Egyptian papyrus in University College London. Senwosret III was one of the great monarchs of the Middle Kingdom, famous for his haggard-looking statues.

50. In ancient Egypt the year consisted of three seasons, the second of which, *Peret*, roughly corresponded to winter (November/February). Crops were sown following the season of the Nile Flood. EA 52947.

51. In 1828 the painter J. M. W. Turner made his third visit to Italy. He left Italy in January and experienced a crossing of the Alps so disastrous that he swore he would never leave so late in winter again. From *Collected Correspondence of J.M.W. Turner, with an Early Diary and Memoir by George Jones*, ed. J. Gage, Oxford, 1980.

52. Turner and his party huddled for warmth en route from Italy. PD 1958-7-12-431 (w. 405). Bequeathed by Robert Wylie Lloyd.

53. From *The Penguin Book of Welsh Verse*, trans. Anthony Conran in assoc. with J. E. Caerwyn Williams, Harmondsworth, 1967.

54. The Dakota (Sioux) recorded the years on hide, paper or cloth by drawing symbols depicting a memorable event for each winter. In this count of the Yanktonai group, associated with Blue Thunder, a scout, camp crier and historian, are 119 pictographs. Ethno Am 7.2 (1942). Given by Miss Smee.

55. This translation captures well the rhythm of Pushkin's original text. From *After Pushkin: Versions of the Poems of Alexander Sergeevich Pushkin by Contemporary Poets*, ed. Elaine Feinstein, Carcanet Press Ltd/The Folio Society, 1999.

56. From a set of eight illustrating various types of Russian sleighs. PD 1895-10-15-88.

57. Translation after J. Lewy, *Revue Hittite et Asianique*, 36 (1938), pp. 122-3.

58. WA 113573.

59. The English version of this game is first recorded in London *c.* 1780. See Iona and Peter Opie (eds), *The Oxford Dictionary of Nursery Rhymes*, Oxford, 1951.

60. PD E.9.163.

61. The telling of riddles, such as these recorded in the *Exeter Book*, was a popular pastime among the Anglo-Saxons. A number of riddles survive, although their solutions are not always clear. The answer to the first riddle here is thought to be 'snow' and to the second 'ice'. From *The Earliest English Poems*, trans. Michael Alexander, Penguin Classics, 3rd edn, Harmondsworth, 1991. © Michael Alexander 1966, 1977, 1991.

62. This screen would have been used as a backdrop to the Tea Ceremony, the image of ice stretching away into the distance providing an illusion of coolness during summer. JA 1982.10-12,01.

63. A song of the people of the Cairns rainforest region of North Queensland, Australia. *Jangala*-style songs describe some intense feeling, or a particularly significant event. Each line in the original text consists of six syllables and the lines may be repeated. From R. M. W. Dixon and Martin Duwell (eds), *The Honey-ant Men's Love Song and Other Aboriginal Song Poems*, University of Queensland Press, 1990.

64. PD 1900-7-25-120-34.

65. Shenstone's family home, The Leasowes, in the parish of Halesowen, Shropshire, was

transformed by him into a *ferme ornée*, an early example of landscape gardening. First published in *The Gentleman's Magazine* 88 (November 1818), the poem is dated 9 January 1747.

66. PD 1947-10-11-3-52.

67. Quarles sided with the royalist cause in the English Civil War but at the same time his moralistic poetry appealed to the Puritans. *The Complete Works . . . of Francis Quarles*, ed. Rev. Alexander B. Grosart, private circulation, 1880.

68. The statue was found at the sanctuary of Demeter at Knidos in south-west Asia Minor (modern Turkey). GR 1859.12-26.26 (Sculpture 1300).

69. Claude McKay was born in Jamaica and emigrated to the USA in 1912, eventually settling in Harlem. Of his work he wrote, 'All my life I have been a troubadour wanderer, nourishing myself mainly on the poetry of existence'. From *Claude McKay, Spring in New Hampshire and Other Poems*, Grant Richards, London, 1920.

70. Queen Victoria retained a deep fondness for the Highlands where she had spent many happy times with her husband, Prince Albert. The card foreshadows a family tragedy. Princess Mary (known as May) became engaged to Albert Victor, Duke of Clarence and Avondale, eldest son of the Prince of Wales, in December 1891, but the Duke died unexpectedly on 14 January 1892. In July 1893, Princess May married his younger brother, later King George V. PD 1947-10-11-2-8.

71. The first known appearance of this traditional carol is in Sir Cuthbert Sharp's *Bishoprick Garland* (1834). From Iona and Peter Opie (eds), *The Oxford Dictionary of Nursery Rhymes*, Oxford, 1951.

72. PD 1933-4-11-154.

73. This text, from a cuneiform tablet in the Library of the Assyrian King Ashurbanipal (r. 668-627 BC), may record the routine of a buffoon or jester. The performer cracks a variety of jokes, some of them presumably of *double entendre*, and an unappetizing religious diet is prescribed. From Benjamin R. Foster, *Before the Muses: An Anthology of Akkadian Literature*, vol. II: *Mature; Late*, CDL Press, Bethesda, MD, 1993.

74. In winter, in the *Tsetseka*, the ceremonial or supernatural season, the peoples of the Northwest Coast of America lived in permanent village settlements away from the sea. The fool dancer was an important figure in their ceremonies and enforced correct behaviour. Ethno Am 2.145 (1944). Given by Mrs H. G. Beazley.

75. Charles Mungoshi, novelist, short story writer and poet, was born into a farming family in Zimbabwe in 1947. He has produced works both in Shona and English. From *The Milkman Doesn't Only Deliver Milk. Poems by Charles Mungoshi selected by Nick Alexander*, The Poetry Society of Zimbabwe, Avondale, 1981 (© Charles Mungoshi).

76. The box, with its winter scene, was designed to contain scarlet paste for the stamping of seal signatures. OA 1991.5-29.1.

77. From *Fantasticks*, London, 1626. Educated at Oxford, Breton later settled in London.

He produced a miscellaneous collection of satirical, religious, romantic and political writing in verse and prose.

78. From a series 'The Four Seasons', depicting women dressed according to the time of year. In the background is Cornhill, London; on the right, the tower of the first Royal Exchange. Hollar was born in Prague and accompanied the Earl of Arundel to London in 1636. PD 1850-2-23-434.

79. Frank O'Connor (1903-66) made available in English some of the finest early poems from Ireland. From *The Penguin Book of Irish Verse*, ed. Brendan Kennelly, Harmondsworth, 1970, 2nd edn, 1981. Reprinted by permission of PFD on behalf of the Estate of Frank O'Connor. © 1970 Frank O'Connor.

80. OA 1995.10-12.02. Given by the artist.

81. The birthday of Scotland's national poet, Robert Burns, is still celebrated with haggis, neeps, tatties and whisky on 25 January. From *The Poetical Works of Robert Burns, the Ayrshire Bard*, Jones & Co., London, 1829. The chorus is old.

82. PD 1985-11-9-47. Given by the British Museum Friends.

83. This poem has sometimes been attributed to King Henry VIII, who was an accomplished musician and poet. British Library, Add. MS 31922, f. 37b. This version is from *Medieval English Lyrics: A Critical Anthology*, ed. R.T. Davies, Faber, London, 1963.

84. PD 1897-5-5-460, vol. V, 60.

Every effort has been made to trace the copyright owners of quoted extracts. The publishers apologize for any errors or omissions in the above list, and would be grateful to be informed of corrections for incorporation in future printings.

ACKNOWLEDGEMENTS

Thanks are due to the following for their advice and assistance:

Isabel Andrews, Michèle Bird, Jill Black, Richard Blurton, Sheila Canby, Tim Clark, Dominique Collon, Kai Dose, Donato Esposito, Teresa Francis, George Hart, Geoffrey House, Jonathan King, Alasdair Macleod, Sheila O'Connell, Richard Parkinson, Jean Rankine, Chris Spring, Lindsay Stainton, Christopher Walker, Beatriz Waters, Sir David Wilson.